From Employee To
Employpreneur

A Guide to Building Your Side Hustle

John Patrick Isiaka

First published in 2024 by
Bironote Enterprise Ltd
Lagos - Nigeria.

www.bironote.com
+2348026596470
info@bironote.com

Copyright @ John Patrick Isiaka 2024

The right of John Patrick Isiaka to be identified as the Author of this Work has been asserted by him in accordance with the Copyright, Design and Patents Act, 1988.

This book is sold subject to the condition that it shall not , by way of trade or otherwise, be lent, resold, hired out or otherwise circulated without the publisher's prior written consent in any form of binding or cover other than that in which it is published and without a similar condition including this condition being imposed on the subsequent purchaser.

A catalogue record for this book is available from the Amazon Online Store.

Table Of Contents

Introduction — 1

Chapter 1: Understanding the Employpreneur Mindset — 3

Chapter 2: Finding Your Side Hustle Idea — 15

Chapter 3: Planning Your Side Business — 21

Chapter 4: Building Your Brand — 27

Chapter 5: Managing Finances and Legalities — 34

Chapter 6: Scaling Your Side Hustle — 40

Chapter 7: Overcoming Challenges and Staying Motivated — 46

Chapter 8: Overcoming Challenges and Staying Motivated — 52

Introduction

"From Employee to Employpreneur: A Guide to Building Your Side Hustle" is a practical and insightful book that serves as a roadmap for individuals looking to transition from being an employee to becoming an employpreneur.

Authored by experts in entrepreneurship and business development, this book provides valuable guidance on how to start and grow a successful side hustle while maintaining a full-time job.

Packed with actionable strategies, real-life examples, and step-by-step advice, this book empowers readers to pursue their entrepreneurial dreams and create additional sources of income. Whether you're looking to supplement your current income, explore your passion projects, or eventually transition into full-time entrepreneurship,

"From Employee to Employpreneur" is the ultimate resource to help you navigate the journey towards building a thriving side hustle.

Chapter 1
Understanding the Employpreneur Mindset

Chapter 1:
Understanding the Employpreneur Mindset

What is an Employpreneur?

In today's ever-evolving job market, the term "Employpreneur" has gained traction as a new way of approaching work and career development. But what exactly does it mean to be an Employpreneur? Simply put, an Employpreneur is someone who takes on the mindset and characteristics of an entrepreneur while still being employed by a traditional company. This individual is not content with simply clocking in and out of work each day, but instead seeks to create additional streams of income and opportunities for growth outside of their regular job.

One of the key traits of an Employpreneur is their ability to think outside the box and identify opportunities for side hustles and additional income streams. Whether it's starting a freelance business, selling products online, or offering consulting services in their field of expertise, Employpreneurs are always on the lookout for ways to diversify their income and expand their skill set.

By taking this proactive approach to their career, Employpreneurs are able to create more stability and security for themselves in an ever-changing economy. Another important aspect of being an Employpreneur is the willingness to take risks and step outside of their comfort zone. Unlike traditional employees who may be content to stay in their current role for years on end, Employpreneurs are constantly seeking new challenges and opportunities for growth. This mindset allows them to stay ahead of the curve and adapt to the changing demands of the job market, ensuring that they are always one step ahead of the competition.

Employpreneurs also understand the importance of building a strong personal brand and network in order to succeed in their side hustle endeavors. By leveraging their existing skills and connections from their day job, Employpreneurs are able to create a solid foundation for their side businesses and attract clients and customers more easily. This strategic approach to networking and branding not only helps Employpreneurs grow their side hustles, but also enhances their overall career prospects and opportunities for advancement in their current job.

Overall, being an Employpreneur is about taking control of your career and creating the opportunities you want to see in your professional life. By combining the entrepreneurial mindset with the stability of a traditional job, Employpreneurs are able to build a successful and fulfilling career on their own terms. Whether you're just starting out in your career or looking to make a change, embracing the Employpreneur mindset can help you achieve your goals and create a more fulfilling and rewarding professional life.

The Benefits of Being an Employpreneur

As an employee who is looking to start their own side hustle, there are numerous benefits to becoming an employpreneur. One of the main advantages is the ability to create multiple streams of income. By starting a side hustle, you can diversify your sources of revenue and reduce your dependence on a single paycheck. This can provide you with a sense of financial security and stability, as well as the opportunity to increase your overall income.

Another benefit of being an employpreneur is the opportunity to pursue your passions and interests outside of your day job. Many employees find that their side hustle allows them to explore their creative side, develop new skills, and engage in activities that bring them joy and fulfillment. This can lead to increased job satisfaction and a greater sense of purpose in both your personal and professional life.

Employpreneurship also offers the chance to build a valuable network of contacts and connections. By engaging with customers, suppliers, and other entrepreneurs in your industry, you can expand your network and open up new opportunities for collaboration and growth. This can lead to increased visibility and credibility in your field, as well as potential partnerships and joint ventures that can help you grow your side hustle into a successful business.

In addition to the financial and personal benefits, being an employpreneur can also provide you with valuable skills and experience that can enhance your career as an employee. By managing your own business, you can develop important skills such as time management, budgeting, marketing, and customer service. These skills can be transferred to your day job and make you a more valuable and versatile employee, increasing your chances of advancement and success in your career.

Overall, becoming an employpreneur can be a rewarding and fulfilling experience for employees who are looking to take control of their financial future and pursue their passions. By starting a side hustle, you can create multiple streams of income, explore your interests, build a valuable network, and develop important skills that can benefit both your side hustle and your career. If you are considering starting your own business, employpreneurship may be the right path for you.

Overcoming Common Myths and Misconceptions

In the world of entrepreneurship, there are many myths and misconceptions that can hold individuals back from pursuing their dreams of building a successful side hustle. In this subchapter, I will address some of the most common myths and misconceptions and provide strategies for overcoming them.

One common myth is that you need a large amount of money to start a side hustle. While having capital can certainly be helpful, there are many low-cost or even free ways to start a business. By utilizing resources like social media, online marketplaces, and networking opportunities, you can launch a side hustle with minimal financial investment.

Another misconception is that you need to quit your job to pursue your side hustle full-time. In reality, many successful entrepreneurs started their businesses while working a full-time job. By creating a solid plan, managing your time effectively, and setting realistic goals, you can build your side hustle while still maintaining your regular employment.

Some individuals believe that entrepreneurship is only for those with a specific skill set or background. The truth is, anyone can become an entrepreneur with the right mindset and determination. By identifying your strengths, seeking out mentorship, and continuously learning and growing, you can develop the skills needed to succeed as an employpreneur.

One of the biggest myths surrounding entrepreneurship is that success happens overnight. Building a successful side hustle takes time, dedication, and perseverance. It is important to set realistic expectations, be patient with yourself, and stay committed to your goals even when faced with challenges or setbacks.

In conclusion, by overcoming common myths and misconceptions about entrepreneurship, you can pave the way for a successful side hustle. By taking a strategic approach, utilizing available resources, and staying focused on your goals, you can transform from an employee to an employpreneur with confidence and determination.

Chapter 2
Finding Your Side Hustle Idea

Chapter 2:
Finding Your Side Hustle Idea

Assessing Your Skills and Interests

Before jumping into the world of side hustles and entrepreneurship, it's crucial to take the time to assess your skills and interests. Understanding what you excel at and what you're passionate about will not only help you choose the right side hustle for you but also set you up for success in the long run.

Start by making a list of your skills, both hard and soft. Hard skills are concrete abilities like graphic design or coding, while soft skills are more intangible qualities like communication or leadership. Consider what you've learned in your current job, as well as any hobbies or volunteer work you've done. This will give you a comprehensive view of what you bring to the table.

Next, think about your interests and passions. What do you love to do in your free time? What topics or causes are you passionate about? Your side hustle is much more likely to succeed if it aligns with your interests, as you'll be more motivated to put in the time and effort required to make it successful.

Once you have a clear picture of your skills and interests, start brainstorming potential side hustle ideas that leverage both. For example, if you're a skilled writer who is passionate about environmental issues, you could start a blog or freelance writing business focused on sustainability. Or if you're a talented photographer who loves animals, you could offer pet photography services in your spare time.

Finally, don't be afraid to seek feedback from others. Talk to friends, family, or colleagues about your skills and interests, and ask for their input on potential side hustle ideas. They may offer valuable insights or suggestions that you hadn't considered. Remember, building a successful side hustle is a journey, and taking the time to assess your skills and interests is an important first step on that path.

Identifying Market Opportunities

Identifying Market Opportunities is a crucial step in the process of building your side hustle as an Employpreneur. In order to successfully transition from being an employee to running your own business, you must have a clear understanding of the market you are entering and the opportunities available to you. This subchapter will guide you through the process of identifying market opportunities and help you develop a strategy for capitalizing on them.

One of the first steps in identifying market opportunities is conducting market research. This involves analyzing the industry you are interested in, studying your competitors, and understanding the needs and preferences of your target audience. By gathering information about the market, you can identify gaps in the market that you can fill with your products or services. This research will also help you determine the size of the market and the potential demand for your offerings.

Once you have conducted thorough market research, it is important to evaluate your own strengths and weaknesses. Consider what skills, knowledge, and experiences you possess that can give you a competitive advantage in the market. Identify areas where you may need to improve or acquire new skills in order to succeed. By understanding your own capabilities, you can better position yourself to take advantage of market opportunities that align with your strengths.

In addition to evaluating your own strengths, it is important to consider the trends and changes in the market that may present new opportunities for your business. Keep an eye on industry news, technological advancements, and consumer behavior to stay ahead of the curve. By staying informed and adaptable, you can position yourself to capitalize on emerging market opportunities and stay relevant in a competitive market.

Finally, once you have identified market opportunities and evaluated your own capabilities, it is time to develop a strategy for entering the market. This may involve creating a unique value proposition, defining your target audience, and setting clear goals for your business. By developing a well-thought-out strategy, you can increase your chances of success as an Employpreneur and differentiate yourself from the competition. Remember, identifying market opportunities is just the first step in building your side hustle – it is up to you to take action and turn those opportunities into a successful business venture.

Researching Potential Side Hustle Ideas

Researching potential side hustle ideas is a crucial step in transitioning from employee to employpreneur. Before diving into a new venture, it's essential to thoroughly explore different options to find the right fit for your skills, interests, and market demand. This process involves conducting market research, identifying trends, and assessing your own strengths and weaknesses.

One effective way to research potential side hustle ideas is to start by brainstorming a list of your skills, hobbies, and interests. Consider what you enjoy doing in your free time or what you excel at in your current job. This will help you identify potential business ideas that align with your passions and strengths. Additionally, think about the problems or needs that you or others may have that could be solved with a new product or service.

Once you have a list of potential side hustle ideas, it's important to conduct market research to determine if there is a demand for your product or service. This involves looking at industry trends, competitors, and target demographics to assess the viability of your business idea. You can also reach out to potential customers or conduct surveys to gather valuable feedback and insights.

Another key aspect of researching potential side hustle ideas is assessing your own strengths and weaknesses. Consider what skills you bring to the table and where you may need to improve or seek help. This self-assessment will help you determine if you have the necessary resources and capabilities to successfully launch and grow a side hustle.

In conclusion, researching potential side hustle ideas is a critical first step in building a successful side business. By brainstorming ideas, conducting market research, and assessing your own strengths and weaknesses, you can identify a profitable and sustainable business idea that aligns with your skills and interests. Remember that thorough research and planning are key to transitioning from an employee to an employpreneur.

Chapter 3

Planning Your Side Business

Chapter 3:

Planning Your Side Business

Setting SMART Goals for Your Side Hustle

Setting SMART goals for your side hustle is crucial to ensuring its success and sustainability. SMART goals are Specific, Measurable, Achievable, Relevant, and Time-bound. By following these guidelines, you can create goals that are clear, actionable, and realistic.

When setting specific goals for your side hustle, it is important to be detailed and precise about what you want to achieve. For example, instead of setting a vague goal like "increase sales," you could set a specific goal like "increase monthly sales by 20% within the next six months." This gives you a clear target to work towards and makes it easier to track your progress.

Measurable goals are important because they allow you to track your progress and see how close you are to achieving your objectives. By setting measurable goals, you can easily identify what is working well and what areas need improvement. This can help you make strategic decisions and adjustments to ensure the success of your side hustle.

Achievable goals are realistic and within reach based on your current resources, skills, and capabilities. Setting goals that are too ambitious or unattainable can lead to frustration and burnout. By setting achievable goals, you can build momentum and confidence as you make progress towards your ultimate vision for your side hustle.

Relevant goals are aligned with your long-term vision and objectives for your side hustle. It is important to ensure that your goals are meaningful and contribute to the overall success and growth of your business. By setting relevant goals, you can stay focused on what truly matters and avoid getting distracted by tasks that do not move you closer to your ultimate goals.

Finally, setting time-bound goals gives you a deadline to work towards and helps you prioritize your tasks and activities. By setting deadlines for your goals, you can create a sense of urgency and motivation to take action. This can help you stay on track and make steady progress towards achieving your goals for your side hustle. By setting SMART goals for your side hustle, you can create a roadmap for success and take your business to the next level.

Creating a Business Plan

Creating a business plan is a crucial step in transitioning from being an employee to becoming an employpreneur. A business plan serves as a roadmap for your side hustle, outlining your goals, strategies, and financial projections. By taking the time to carefully craft a business plan, you are setting yourself up for success and ensuring that your side hustle has a solid foundation to grow and thrive.

When creating a business plan, it is important to start by defining your business idea and identifying your target market. What problem does your side hustle solve? Who are your potential customers? By understanding your target market and their needs, you can tailor your products or services to meet their demands and differentiate yourself from competitors.

Next, you will need to outline your business goals and objectives. What do you hope to achieve with your side hustle? Whether it's generating a certain amount of revenue, reaching a specific number of customers, or expanding into new markets, setting clear and measurable goals will help you stay focused and motivated as you work towards building your business.

In addition to setting goals, your business plan should also include a detailed marketing strategy. How will you promote your products or services and attract customers? Will you use social media, digital marketing, or other advertising channels? By outlining your marketing tactics and budget in your business plan, you can ensure that you are effectively reaching your target audience and driving sales for your side hustle.

Finally, your business plan should include financial projections and a budget for your side hustle. How much money do you need to get started? What are your projected expenses and revenues for the first year? By creating a realistic financial plan, you can ensure that you have the resources necessary to launch and grow your side hustle successfully.

Overall, creating a business plan is a critical step in building your side hustle as an employpreneur. By defining your business idea, setting goals, developing a marketing strategy, and creating financial projections, you can establish a strong foundation for your side hustle and increase your chances of long-term success.

Managing Your Time Effectively

Managing your time effectively is crucial when building your side hustle as an employpreneur. As an employee with limited hours outside of your full-time job, it's essential to maximize the time you have available to work on your passion project. By implementing time management strategies, you can ensure that you are making progress towards your goals without sacrificing your personal or professional life.

One key aspect of managing your time effectively is setting clear goals and priorities. Identify the most important tasks that will move your side hustle forward and focus on completing them first. This will help you avoid getting overwhelmed by a long to-do list and ensure that you are making meaningful progress towards your goals.

Another important aspect of time management is creating a schedule and sticking to it. Set aside dedicated time each day or week to work on your side hustle, and treat this time as you would any other important commitment. By establishing a routine, you can build consistency and momentum in your work, leading to greater productivity and results.

It's also important to eliminate distractions and stay focused during your dedicated work time. Turn off notifications on your phone, find a quiet workspace, and set specific goals for each work session to keep yourself on track. By minimizing distractions and staying focused, you can make the most of the time you have available to work on your side hustle.

In conclusion, managing your time effectively is essential for employpreneurs looking to build their side hustle while working a full-time job. By setting clear goals, creating a schedule, eliminating distractions, and staying focused, you can make the most of your limited time and achieve success in your entrepreneurial endeavors. Remember, every minute counts when it comes to building your dream business, so make the most of the time you have available.

Chapter 4
Building Your Brand

Chapter 4:
Building Your Brand

Defining Your Unique Value Proposition

In the world of entrepreneurship, one of the most important concepts to grasp is that of the unique value proposition. This is essentially what sets your business apart from others in the market and defines why customers should choose your product or service over your competitors. As an employee looking to transition into the world of entrepreneurship, it is crucial to define your unique value proposition early on in order to stand out and attract customers to your side hustle.

Defining your unique value proposition starts with identifying what sets you apart from others in your industry. This could be a unique skill set, a specialized knowledge base, or a different approach to solving a particular problem. By understanding what makes you unique, you can begin to craft a value proposition that highlights these strengths and communicates the benefits of working with you to potential customers.

Once you have identified your unique value proposition, it is important to clearly communicate it to your target audience. This means incorporating it into your marketing materials, website, social media profiles, and any other channels you use to reach customers. By consistently communicating your unique value proposition, you can build brand awareness and attract customers who are looking for the specific benefits you offer.

In addition to communicating your unique value proposition externally, it is also important to integrate it into your business practices and processes. This could mean aligning your pricing strategy with the value you provide, creating products or services that directly address the needs of your target audience, or developing a unique customer experience that sets you apart from competitors. By aligning your entire business around your unique value proposition, you can create a cohesive brand identity that resonates with customers and differentiates you from the competition.

In conclusion, defining your unique value proposition is a critical step in building a successful side hustle as an employee turned employpreneuer. By identifying what sets you apart from others in your industry, clearly communicating it to your target audience, and integrating it into your business practices, you can attract customers, build brand loyalty, and ultimately achieve success in your entrepreneurial endeavors. Remember, your unique value proposition is what makes you stand out in a crowded market - embrace it, communicate it, and let it guide your path to success.

Developing Your Brand Identity

Developing Your Brand Identity is a crucial step in establishing a successful side hustle as an employpreneur. Your brand identity is the essence of your business - it's what sets you apart from your competitors and helps you connect with your target audience on a deeper level. In this subchapter, we will explore the key components of building a strong brand identity that will resonate with your customers and help you stand out in a crowded marketplace.

The first step in developing your brand identity is defining your unique selling proposition (USP). Your USP is what makes your business different from others in your industry and why customers should choose you over your competitors. It could be your expertise in a specific niche, your exceptional customer service, or your innovative products or services. By clearly defining your USP, you can communicate your value proposition to your target audience and attract customers who align with your brand's values.

Once you have defined your USP, you can start to develop your brand's visual identity. This includes creating a logo, choosing a color palette, and selecting fonts that reflect your brand's personality and values. Your visual identity should be consistent across all of your marketing materials, from your website to your social media profiles, to create a cohesive and memorable brand experience for your customers.

In addition to your visual identity, your brand voice is another important aspect of your brand identity. Your brand voice is the tone and style of your communications with your audience, whether it's through your website, social media posts, or email newsletters. Your brand voice should be authentic, consistent, and reflective of your brand's values and personality. By developing a strong brand voice, you can build trust and loyalty with your customers and stand out in a crowded marketplace.

Overall, developing your brand identity is a key component of building a successful side hustle as an employpreneur. By defining your USP, creating a strong visual identity, and developing a consistent brand voice, you can differentiate your business from your competitors and connect with your target audience in a meaningful way. Remember, your brand identity is not just about your logo or color scheme - it's about the story you tell, the values you uphold, and the relationships you build with your customers.

Marketing Your Side Business

When it comes to building your side hustle, marketing is key to attracting customers and growing your business. In this subchapter, I will also explore various strategies and tactics you can use to effectively market your side business and reach your target audience. Whether you are a full-time employee looking to supplement your income or a budding entrepreneur with a passion project on the side, these marketing tips will help you take your business to the next level.

The first step in marketing your side business is to define your target audience. Who are the people that would benefit from your products or services? What are their needs, preferences, and pain points? By understanding your target audience, you can tailor your marketing efforts to reach and resonate with them. Conduct market research, create customer personas, and analyze your competitors to gain insights into your target audience and how to effectively reach them.

Once you have identified your target audience, it's time to create a marketing plan. Your marketing plan should outline your goals, target audience, strategies, tactics, budget, and timeline. Consider which marketing channels are most effective for reaching your target audience, such as out-of-home signs, radio jinge, TV commercial, print advertising, social media, email marketing, content marketing, influencer marketing, or paid advertising. Develop a content calendar and schedule to ensure consistency in your marketing efforts and maximize your reach.

In addition to digital marketing, consider offline marketing strategies to promote your side business. Attend networking events, trade shows, and conferences to connect with potential customers and partners. Collaborate with other businesses or influencers in your niche to reach a wider audience. Utilize traditional marketing tactics such as flyers, brochures, business cards, and direct mail to raise awareness of your side business in your local community.

As you implement your marketing plan, track and measure the results of your efforts. Use analytics tools to monitor the performance of your marketing campaigns, such as website traffic, social media engagement, email open rates, and sales conversions. Analyze the data to identify what is working well and what areas need improvement. Adjust your marketing strategies accordingly to optimize your results and achieve your business goals.

Remember that marketing is an ongoing process that requires constant monitoring, testing, and refinement. Stay up-to-date on the latest marketing trends and technologies to stay ahead of the competition and continue growing your side business. By following these marketing tips and strategies, you can effectively promote your side business, attract more customers, and achieve success as an employpreneur.

Chapter 5
Managing Finances and Legalities

Chapter 5:

Managing Finances and Legalities

Setting Up Your Business Structure

When transitioning from being an employee to an employpreneur, one of the most important steps you'll need to take is setting up your business structure. This decision will have a significant impact on how your business operates. There are several options to consider, including sole proprietorship, partnership, limited liability company (LLC), and corporation. Each structure has its own advantages and disadvantages, so it's important to carefully consider which one is best for your particular business.

One of the simplest business structures is a sole proprietorship, where you are the sole owner of the business and are personally responsible for all debts and liabilities. This structure is easy to set up and requires minimal paperwork, making it a popular choice for many employpreneurs just starting out. However, one downside of a sole proprietorship is that there is no legal separation between you and your business.

Another option to consider is a partnership, where two or more individuals share ownership of the business. Partnerships can be a good choice if you want to work with someone else to start and grow your business. However, it's important to have a clear partnership agreement in place that outlines each partner's roles, responsibilities, and profit-sharing arrangements. This can help avoid conflicts and misunderstandings down the road.

For employpreneurs looking for more protection against personal liability, forming a limited liability company (LLC) may be a good option. An LLC provides a legal separation between the business and its owners, which can help shield your personal assets from business debts and lawsuits. In addition, an LLC offers flexibility in terms of management structure and taxation, making it a popular choice for many small businesses.

In conclusion, setting up your business structure is a crucial step in transitioning from being an employee to an employpreneur. By carefully considering the advantages and disadvantages of each option, you can choose the right structure that aligns with your business goals, risk tolerance, and long-term vision.

Managing Your Finances

Managing your finances is a crucial aspect of building your side hustle as an employpreneur. It's important to have a clear understanding of your current financial situation in order to make informed decisions about your business ventures.

It's important to have a clear understanding of your current financial situation in order to make informed decisions about your business ventures. One key tip is to create a budget that outlines your income, expenses, and savings goals. By tracking your finances closely, you can identify areas where you can cut costs and allocate more resources towards your side hustle.

Another important aspect of managing your finances as an emplpreneur is setting financial goals. Whether it's saving a certain amount of money each month or reaching a specific revenue target for your side hustle, having clear goals can help you stay motivated and focused on your financial success. It's also important to regularly review and adjust your goals as your financial situation changes.

In addition to setting financial goals, it's essential to establish an emergency fund to cover unexpected expenses or emergencies. This fund should ideally cover three to six months' worth of living expenses and can provide you with peace of mind knowing that you have a financial safety net in place. By prioritizing your emergency fund, you can protect yourself from financial setbacks and focus on growing your side hustle.

As an employpreneur, it's also important to diversify your income streams to reduce your financial risk. Relying solely on your side hustle for income can be risky, especially if the market fluctuates or your business experiences a slowdown. By exploring other income opportunities such as freelancing, consulting, or investing, you can create a more stable financial foundation for yourself and your side hustle.

Overall, managing your finances effectively is a key component of building your side hustle as an employpreneur.

By reating a budget, setting financial goals, establishing an emergency fund, and diversifying your income streams, you can ensure that your financial future is secure and your side hustle has the best chance of success. Remember, financial management is an ongoing process, so be sure to regularly review and adjust your financial strategies as needed.

Understanding Tax Implications

As you embark on your journey from being an employee to an employpreneur, it is important to understand the tax implications that come with running your own side hustle. Many employees who start a side business are unaware of the tax obligations that come with it, which can lead to financial stress and potential penalties from the IRS, FIRS as the case may be. In this subchapter, I will also explore the key tax considerations you need to keep in mind as you build your side hustle.

First and foremost, it is crucial to keep accurate records of all your income and expenses related to your side business. This will not only help you track your profitability but also ensure that you are prepared come tax season. You will need to report your side hustle income on your annual tax return, and having detailed records will make this process much smoother.

Another important tax implication to consider is the classification of your side hustle. Depending on how you structure your business, you may be subject to different tax rates and regulations. For example, if you operate as a sole proprietorship, you will report your business income on your personal tax return and be subject to self-employment taxes.

On the other hand, if you form a limited liability company (LLC) or corporation, you may have different tax obligations and benefits.

In addition to income taxes, employpreneurs must also consider other taxes such as sales tax, payroll tax, and state taxes. These obligations can vary depending on your location and the nature of your business. It is important to research and understand the tax requirements in your area to avoid any surprises down the road.

Furthermore, as an employpreneur, you may be eligible for certain tax deductions and credits that can help lower your overall tax liability. Expenses related to your side business, such as supplies, equipment, and marketing, may be deductible. Additionally, if you use a portion of your home for business purposes, you may be able to deduct a percentage of your mortgage interest, utilities, and other expenses.

In conclusion, understanding the tax implications of running a side hustle is essential for employpreneurs to maintain compliance with the law and maximize their financial success. By keeping accurate records, choosing the right business structure, and taking advantage of available deductions, you can navigate the world of taxes with confidence and ensure that your side hustle remains a profitable venture.

Chapter 6

Scaling Your Side Hustle

Chapter 6:

Scaling Your Side Hustle

Setting Growth Goals

Setting growth goals is a crucial step for anyone looking to transition from being an employee to becoming an employpreneur. As an employpreneur, you are essentially an employee who is also an entrepreneur, managing a side hustle alongside your regular job. In order to grow your side hustle and eventually make it your full-time gig, it is important to set clear and achievable growth goals.

The first step in setting growth goals is to define what success looks like for your side hustle. This could mean reaching a certain level of income, gaining a specific number of clients, or expanding your offerings. By clearly defining your goals, you will have a roadmap to follow and a clear vision of where you want your business to go.

Once you have defined your goals, it is important to break them down into smaller, actionable steps. For example, if your goal is to increase your income by 50% in the next year, you could break that down into monthly targets for sales or client acquisition. By breaking your goals down into smaller steps, you can track your progress more easily and make adjustments as needed.

Another important aspect of setting growth goals is to make sure they are realistic and achievable. While it is important to challenge yourself, setting goals that are too lofty or unrealistic can lead to frustration and burnout. It is better to set smaller, achievable goals that you can build on over time.

Finally, it is important to regularly review and revise your growth goals. As your side hustle evolves and grows, your goals may need to be adjusted to reflect new opportunities or challenges. By regularly reviewing your goals and making adjustments as needed, you can ensure that your side hustle continues to grow and thrive. By setting clear, achievable growth goals and regularly reviewing and revising them, you can take your side hustle from a passion project to a successful business venture.

Hiring Help and Outsourcing Tasks

One of the key aspects of transitioning from being an employee to an employpreneur is learning how to effectively delegate tasks and hire help when needed. As you build your side hustle, you may find that you simply can't do everything on your own. This is where outsourcing tasks can be incredibly valuable. By hiring help, you can free up your time to focus on the aspects of your business that you excel at, while leaving other tasks in the hands of experts.

When it comes to hiring help, it's important to be strategic about where you allocate your resources. Consider which tasks are taking up the most time and which ones could be easily outsourced. For example, administrative tasks such as bookkeeping or social media management can often be outsourced to freelancers or virtual assistants. By freeing up your time from these tasks, you can focus on growing your business and generating more revenue.

Outsourcing tasks can also help you scale your business more quickly. As your side hustle grows, you may find that you simply can't keep up with the demand on your own. By hiring help, you can take on more clients or customers and expand your services without becoming overwhelmed. This can help you reach your financial goals faster and achieve greater success in your employpreneur journey.

When hiring help, be sure to clearly communicate your expectations and provide detailed instructions for the tasks at hand. This will help ensure that the work is completed to your satisfaction and that you get the results you're looking for. Additionally, be prepared to invest time in training and onboarding any new hires to ensure they understand your business and its goals. By setting clear expectations and providing support, you can build a strong team of freelancers or employees who can help you achieve your employpreneur dreams.

In conclusion, hiring help and outsourcing tasks can be a game-changer for employpreneurs looking to grow their side hustles. By delegating tasks to experts and focusing on what you do best, you can free up your time to scale your business and achieve greater success. Remember to be strategic in your hiring decisions, communicate clearly with your team, and invest in training and onboarding to set yourself up for success. With the right support in place, you can take your side hustle to new heights and build a thriving employpreneur business.

Expanding Your Product or Service Offerings

Expanding Your Product or Service Offerings is a crucial step in growing your side hustle and transitioning from being an employee to an employpreneur.

By diversifying what you offer, you can attract a wider range of customers and increase your revenue streams. In this subchapter, I will explore different strategies for expanding your product or service offerings and how to effectively market them to your target audience.

One way to expand your offerings is to look at what complementary products or services you can add to your current lineup. For example, if you are a freelance graphic designer, you could consider offering website design services or branding packages to your clients. By expanding into related areas, you can tap into new markets and attract clients who may have different needs than your current customer base.

Another strategy for expanding your offerings is to listen to your customers and identify any gaps in the market that you could fill. Conducting surveys, talking to your current clients, and staying up-to-date on industry trends can help you identify new opportunities for growth. For example, if you run a meal prep service and notice that many of your customers are asking for gluten-free options, you could consider adding a gluten-free menu to your offerings.

When expanding your product or service offerings, it's important to communicate these changes effectively to your target audience. Use your website, social media channels, and email marketing to promote your new offerings and explain the benefits to your customers. Consider offering special promotions or discounts to incentivize customers to try out your new products or services.

By diversifying what you offer, you can attract a wider range of customers and increase your revenue streams. In this subchapter, I will explore different strategies for expanding your product or service offerings and how to effectively market them to your target audience.

One way to expand your offerings is to look at what complementary products or services you can add to your current lineup. For example, if you are a freelance graphic designer, you could consider offering website design services or branding packages to your clients. By expanding into related areas, you can tap into new markets and attract clients who may have different needs than your current customer base.

Another strategy for expanding your offerings is to listen to your customers and identify any gaps in the market that you could fill. Conducting surveys, talking to your current clients, and staying up-to-date on industry trends can help you identify new opportunities for growth. For example, if you run a meal prep service and notice that many of your customers are asking for gluten-free options, you could consider adding a gluten-free menu to your offerings.

When expanding your product or service offerings, it's important to communicate these changes effectively to your target audience. Use your website, social media channels, and email marketing to promote your new offerings and explain the benefits to your customers. Consider offering special promotions or discounts to incentivize customers to try out your new products or services.

Finally, remember that expanding your offerings is a continuous process. Stay open to feedback from your customers and be willing to adapt and evolve your offerings based on their needs and preferences. By continually innovating and expanding your product or service lineup, you can stay ahead of the competition and build a successful side hustle as an employpreneur.

Chapter 7
Overcoming Challenges and Staying Motivated

Chapter 7:
Overcoming Challenges and Staying Motivated

Dealing with Setbacks and Failures

Dealing with setbacks and failures is an inevitable part of the journey to becoming an employpreneur. It's important to remember that setbacks are not a sign of failure, but rather an opportunity for growth and learning. When faced with a setback, it's crucial to remain resilient and determined to push through.

One of the key ways to deal with setbacks is to adopt a growth mindset. Instead of viewing setbacks as obstacles, see them as opportunities to learn and improve. Reflect on what went wrong and what you can do differently next time. By embracing a growth mindset, you can turn setbacks into stepping stones towards success.

It's also important to seek support during times of setbacks. Whether it's from friends, family, or a mentor, having a strong support system can help you navigate through tough times. Surround yourself with positive and encouraging people who believe in your potential and can offer valuable advice and perspective.

Another way to deal with setbacks is to stay focused on your goals and vision. Remind yourself of why you started your side hustle in the first place and the impact you want to make. By staying focused on your long-term vision, you can overcome setbacks with a renewed sense of purpose and determination.

Lastly, remember that setbacks are a normal part of the entrepreneurial journey. Every successful employpreneur has faced setbacks and failures along the way. What sets them apart is their ability to bounce back and keep moving forward. By embracing setbacks as learning opportunities and staying focused on your goals, you can navigate through challenges and come out stronger on the other side.

Building a Support Network

Building a support network is crucial when it comes to transitioning from being an employee to becoming an employpreneur. As you embark on this exciting journey of building your side hustle, having a strong support system in place can make all the difference in your success. Your support network can provide you with guidance, motivation, and encouragement when you face challenges and setbacks along the way.

One of the first steps in building a support network is identifying the people in your life who believe in your vision and are willing to support you in your entrepreneurial endeavors. This could be friends, family members, colleagues, or mentors who understand your goals and are willing to offer their advice and assistance. Surrounding yourself with positive and like-minded individuals can help you stay focused and motivated as you work towards building your side hustle.

Networking is another important aspect of building a support network as an employpreneur. By connecting with other entrepreneurs, professionals, and industry experts, you can gain valuable insights, resources, and opportunities that can help you grow your side hustle. Attending networking events, joining online communities, and participating in industry-related workshops are great ways to expand your network and establish meaningful connections with others who can support you on your journey.

In addition to building a support network of individuals, it's also important to cultivate relationships with organizations and resources that can provide you with the tools and support you need to succeed as an employpreneur. This could include joining coworking spaces, enrolling in entrepreneurship programs, or seeking out business incubators and accelerators that can help you develop your side hustle and take it to the next level. By leveraging these resources, you can access valuable expertise, funding, and opportunities that can propel your entrepreneurial venture forward.

Ultimately, building a strong support network is about surrounding yourself with people and resources that can help you navigate the challenges and uncertainties of building a side hustle. By cultivating relationships with individuals who believe in your vision, networking with industry professionals, and leveraging organizational resources, you can create a solid foundation of support that will empower you to succeed as an employpreneur. Remember, you don't have to go it alone – with the right support network in place, you can achieve your entrepreneurial goals and build a successful side hustle that aligns with your passions and aspirations.

Maintaining a Healthy Work-Life Balance

Maintaining a healthy work-life balance is crucial for anyone looking to build a successful side hustle while still holding down a full-time job. In today's fast-paced world, it can be easy to get caught up in the hustle and bustle of work, leaving little time for personal life and self-care. However, finding a balance between work and personal life is essential for both your mental and physical well-being.

One of the first steps to maintaining a healthy work-life balance is to set boundaries between work and personal time. This means establishing specific work hours and sticking to them, as well as carving out time for relaxation, hobbies, and social activities. It's important to prioritize self-care and ensure that you are taking care of your physical and mental health in order to avoid burnout.

In addition to setting boundaries, it's important to prioritize tasks and manage your time effectively. This means being mindful of how you spend your time and making sure that you are focusing on activities that are important and align with your goals. By prioritizing tasks and managing your time effectively, you can avoid feeling overwhelmed and ensure that you are making progress on your side hustle without sacrificing your personal life.

Another key component of maintaining a healthy work-life balance is learning to say no. It can be tempting to take on more work than you can handle, especially when building a side hustle on top of a full-time job. However, it's important to recognize your limits and not overcommit yourself. Learning to say no to tasks or projects that don't align with your goals or values can help you maintain a healthy balance between work and personal life.

Overall, maintaining a healthy work-life balance is essential for anyone looking to build a successful side hustle while still holding down a full-time job. By setting boundaries, prioritizing tasks, managing your time effectively, and learning to say no, you can ensure that you are taking care of your physical and mental well-being while also making progress on your side hustle. Remember, a healthy work-life balance is key to long-term success and happiness in both your personal and professional life.

Chapter 8
Transitioning from Employee to Full-Time Employpreneur

Chapter 8:
Transitioning from Employee to Full-Time Employpreneur

Knowing When to Make the Jump

Knowing when to make the jump from being an employee to becoming an employpreneur is a crucial decision that requires careful consideration and planning. Many individuals dream of starting their own side hustle or business, but knowing when the right time is can be tricky. This subchapter aims to provide guidance and insights on how to determine when it's time to take the leap and pursue your entrepreneurial ambitions.

One key indicator that it may be time to make the jump is when you find yourself feeling unfulfilled or stagnant in your current job. If you constantly daydream about starting your own business and feel a burning passion for a particular idea or project, it may be a sign that you are ready to make the transition. Trusting your instincts and recognizing your true desires is essential in determining when the time is right to pursue your employpreneurial goals.

Another important factor to consider when deciding to make the jump is your financial stability. It's crucial to have a solid financial plan in place before leaving your job to pursue your side hustle full-time. Consider creating a budget, saving up an emergency fund, and exploring potential sources of funding or investment to support your business as it grows. Being financially prepared will give you the peace of mind and security needed to take the leap confidently.

Additionally, assessing your skills, experience, and network can help you determine if you are ready to become an employpreneur. Reflect on your strengths, weaknesses, and areas of expertise to identify where you can add value and differentiate yourself in the market. Leveraging your existing skills and connections can help you establish a strong foundation for your business and increase your chances of success as an employpreneur.

Lastly, seeking support and guidance from mentors, advisors, and fellow employpreneurs can be invaluable in helping you make the jump successfully. Surround yourself with like-minded individuals who can offer advice, encouragement, and resources to support you on your entrepreneurial journey. Building a strong support network can provide you with the motivation, inspiration, and knowledge needed to navigate the challenges of starting and growing your side hustle.

In conclusion, knowing when to make the jump from being an employee to becoming an employpreneur is a personal decision that requires careful consideration and planning. By assessing your passion, financial stability, skills, and support system, you can determine when the time is right to pursue your entrepreneurial ambitions. Trust your instincts, be prepared, and seek guidance from those who have walked the same path to help you make a successful transition to employpreneurship.

Planning for a Smooth Transition

Transitioning from being an employee to becoming an employpreneur can be a daunting process, but with proper planning, it can be a smooth and successful journey. Planning for a smooth transition involves setting clear goals, creating a timeline, and developing a solid business plan. By taking the time to carefully plan out your transition, you can avoid common pitfalls and set yourself up for success as you embark on your new entrepreneurial journey.

One of the first steps in planning for a smooth transition is to set clear goals for your employpreneurial venture. Consider what you hope to achieve with your side hustle and how it aligns with your long-term aspirations. By defining your goals, you can create a roadmap for your transition and stay focused on what you want to accomplish. Whether your goal is to supplement your income, pursue a passion project, or eventually transition to full-time entrepreneurship, having a clear vision will help guide your decisions and actions.

Creating a timeline for your transition is another important aspect of planning for a smooth shift from employee to employpreneur. Consider how much time you can realistically dedicate to your side hustle each week and set milestones for when you hope to achieve certain goals. Having a timeline will help you stay on track and hold yourself accountable as you work towards building your business. Be sure to factor in any potential obstacles or challenges that may arise along the way and adjust your timeline accordingly to stay on course.

Developing a solid business plan is essential for any employpreneur looking to make a successful transition from employee to entrepreneur. Your business plan should outline your business idea, target market, pricing strategy, marketing plan, and financial projections. By taking the time to create a comprehensive business plan, you can identify potential risks and opportunities, as well as set realistic goals for your employpreneurial venture. A well-thought-out business plan will not only help guide your actions but also serve as a valuable tool for attracting investors or securing financing if needed.

In conclusion, planning for a smooth transition from employee to employpreneur requires careful consideration and strategic thinking. By setting clear goals, creating a timeline, and developing a solid business plan, you can increase your chances of success and make the transition as smooth as possible. Remember that transitioning to employpreneurship is a journey, and it is important to be patient and persistent as you work towards building your side hustle. With the right planning and mindset, you can successfully transition from employee to employpreneur and achieve your entrepreneurial goals.

When setting new goals for your side hustle, consider both short-term and long-term objectives that align with your overall vision and mission. Whether you aim to increase your client base, launch a new product or service, or expand into new markets, setting clear and measurable goals will help you stay on track and ensure continued success. Remember to break down your goals into smaller, manageable tasks that you can work towards each day to steadily progress towards achieving them.

In conclusion, celebrating your success and setting new goals are essential practices for employpreneurs looking to build their side hustle. Taking the time to recognize and appreciate your accomplishments not only boosts your morale and motivation but also sets the stage for continued growth and success. By setting new goals that align with your vision and mission, you can stay focused, motivated, and on track towards building a successful and fulfilling side hustle.

John Patrick Isiaka is a seasoned entrepreneur, author, and speaker with a passion for helping individuals transition from being employees to becoming employpreneurs. With a background in business development and a track record of successfully building side hustles, John brings a wealth of knowledge and experience to his book **"From Employee to Employpreneur: A Guide to Building Your Side Hustle."** Having navigated the challenges of starting and growing his own side businesses, John understands the struggles and uncertainties that aspiring employpreneurs face. Through his writing and speaking engagements, he aims to empower others to pursue their entrepreneurial dreams while still maintaining their primary source of income. John's practical advice, actionable strategies, and motivational insights make him a trusted resource for individuals looking to create additional streams of income and achieve financial independence. His book serves as a roadmap for those who are ready to take the leap into entrepreneurship and build a successful side hustle. With a genuine desire to see others succeed, John Patrick Isiaka continues to inspire and guide aspiring employpreneurs on their journey to financial freedom and fulfillment.

www.ingramcontent.com/pod-product-compliance
Lightning Source LLC
Chambersburg PA
CBHW070419230526
45471CB00006B/2882